THE HUMID TROPICS

Alan and Enid have around 10,000 plants to choose from in the Humid Tropics Biome.

TROPIC TRADER

Jot down the name of the ship. It may help me out later!

....

WELCOME TO THE HUMID TROPICS!

THE HUMID TROPICS BIOME

In the tropical Biome it's hot (between 18°C and 35°C) and damp (around 70% relative humidity) – just like being in a rainforest! You'll find tropical places near the equator on a map.

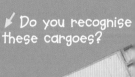

TROPICAL PLANTS FOR YOU

Take a close look at the crates on the ship. Sugar, coffee and bananas all come from the tropics. So do chocolate (from cocoa beans) and chewing gum (from chicle trees).

↙ Do you recognise these cargoes?

YOUR JOURNEY STARTS THIS WAY ←

↑Tropical plants had to be brought across the sea.

CRUDE RUBBER

OIL

BLACK-BAKE CRUDE RUBBER

BANANAS

2

If we were ancient Egyptians we'd be looking for PAPYRUS to write on. Which plant is it?

Where's the TRAVELLER'S PALM to point us in the right direction?

H.01

PAPYRUS (H.01)

On both sides of the path you'll see huge clumps of the tall papyrus plant. The ancient Egyptians used the white pith inside the stems to make a kind of paper for writing on. We get our word 'paper' from it.

↑ Papyrus plants.

TRAVELLER'S PALM (H.01)

The massive palms with stems that look like huge fans are called Traveller's palms because the line of the stems points from east to west.

↓ Traveller's palm.

DIGGER FACTS!

DIGGER'S RAINFOREST FACTS

Birdsong
There are twenty small, green birds called Sulawesi White Eyes in the Biome to eat the bugs that could damage the plants.

Wooden store cupboards
Rainforest trees suck carbon dioxide out of the air and turn it into ... wood. Good news, as high levels of carbon dioxide can contribute to global warming.

LET'S VISIT SOME ISLANDS...

THE TROPICAL ISLANDS
(H.02)

Isolated islands are homes for many unusual plants. The plants are endangered when people build on the land and introduce fast-growing crops that take over.

THE MANGROVES (H.02)

Mangrove forests grow in the tidal mud between land and sea. Look out for the 'snorkels' that are above the ground to allow the plants to breathe even when the tide is in.

↑ View across the island lake.

↑ Young mangroves.

DIGGER FACTS!

DIGGER'S ISLAND FACTS

Biggest seed in the world is the bottom-like coco-de-mer seed, from a palm that grows naturally only in the Seychelles.

Balsamine sauvage
This rare plant is only found on two islands in the Seychelles. Eden scientists are working with people there to save it from extinction.

4

Wood from MANGROVE trees would give them timber and fuel.

Can you find a fruit named after something that twinkles in the sky?

....

... AND MALAYSIA

MALAYSIAN HOUSE (H.03)

Raised on stilts to keep out water and snakes, this house is mainly made from plants, including wood from the surrounding trees, bamboo and rattan (a prickly climbing palm).

↑ Hot chillies.

KEBUN: THE HOME GARDEN (H.03)

Houses in Malaysia have fantastic gardens with a bit of everything right outside the door: nutritious fruit and vegetables all year round, spices, such as hot chillies (paprika), and herbs for food and medicine.

The useful horse-radish tree (or moringa tree) has edible leaves, flowers, beans and roots, with seeds that can be pressed for oil.

↑ Malaysian house with kitchen garden.

↑ Horseradish or 'miracle' tree.

I'm looking for CASSAVA ROOTS. The leaves of this plant are like fingers.

I need PAPAYAS and MANGOS for the fruit bowl.

FROM WEST AFRICA TO...

WEST AFRICA. AGROFORESTRY SYSTEMS (H.04)

Papayas, mangos and other tall fruit trees can be planted in a forest garden to give welcome shade to shorter crop plants below. When everything gets overgrown, great ... a new bit of rainforest is born.

↑ Mangos on the tree.

↑ Papaya tree and fruit.

↑ Alley-cropping on a steep slope.

Look for the tallest tree in the Biome (just into South America, on the left). What is its name?

....

ALLEY CROPPING (H.04)

How do you grow crops on steep slopes? Here (in season) maize is planted along the contours between lines of trees and vetiver grass. The roots help to prevent the soil falling down the slope.

Help Alan and Enid find some WATER CHESTNUT TREES (they look a bit like conker trees).

LOWER ROAD PAST THE COOL REST ROOM TO THE POST THAT SAYS SOUTH AMERICA.

... TROPICAL SOUTH AMERICA

MOBILE GARDENS (H.05)

In the forest, patches are cleared for food crops such as cassava and sweet potatoes. Each year the garden is moved to a new plot and the old garden becomes forest again.

↑ Cassava plant.

WILD HARVEST (H.05)

The rainforest itself is like a wild garden for the people who live in it. They can harvest water chestnuts, wild fruits, and honey made by wild bees. All sorts of other wild plants are picked for food, fuel, medicine and building materials.

↑ Water chestnut tree by river.

DIGGER FACTS!

DIGGER'S HUMID TROPICS BIOME FACTS

Where does the water come from? At Eden rainwater and ground water draining into the pit are used to top up the waterfall.

Hidden Peruvian paintings
On the top path up near the waterfall are some paintings by Yolanda Panduro Baneo and Francisco Montes Shuna, a shaman (a medicine man), from Peru.

Which tree did our COLA DRINK come from?

H.06

H.07

H.07

H.08

RAINFOREST TREATS

↑ This side of the arch shows you the plants.

CROPS AND CULTIVATION ARCH (H.06)

Take a look at the arch. On one side are the plants, and on the other are the products. Can you see which goes with what?

I've found my long lost brother! Write down what's engraved on the pillar beneath him.

....

↑ Cola tree.

↑ Products on the other side.

COLA (H.07) AND GUM (H.08)

Cola drinks were first made from the nut of the cola tree, Cola acuminata.

Chewing gum used to be made from the milky liquid, chicle, collected from the trunk of the sapodilla tree.

↑ Sapodilla tree.

8

What we really need is RUBBER for tyres and rubber gloves and TIMBER for the table.

H.09

Can you find the trees that gave us CHEWING GUM?

ARTIFICE **H.10**

RUBBER TREES
(H.09)

Rubber is made from a white sticky liquid, called latex, that comes out of the rubber tree. The rubber tapper cuts the tree carefully and collects the latex in a cup tied to the tree.

↑ Latex being collected.

BOING! (H.09)

In Malaysia, Indonesia and other tropical countries millions of rubber trees have been planted to provide rubber for tyres, soles of shoes, sports equipment, rubber bands and more.

↙ The rubber exhibit.

RUBBER · BLUBBER · BOUNCE · FLOUNCE · WIND IT · STRETCH IT · THROW IT · SIT ON IT · RUB OUT WITH IT · WEAR IT · TEAR IT · LOVE IT!!

NATURAL RUBBER IS... ·RUBBER RULES OK·

DIGGER FACTS!

DIGGER DIGGING ON TIMBER
Did you know?

Rainforest trees can end up as front doors and tables. Digger found out that this was not so bad if they were cut down without wrecking the surrounding forest.

Did you know?

In forests that are well looked after, trees are cut down carefully. Only a few trees are cut down at a time and new trees are planted in their place. Look out for products with approved labels, such as the Forestry Stewardship Council label (FSC).

FSC

COCONUT PALMS are easy to spot, but what do CHOCOLATE trees look like?

I'd rather find the plants for COOKING OIL.

H.11

HOW DOES CHOCOLATE GROW?

COCOA (H.11)

When the big, green pods on the trunks ripen to orange they are cut off and opened. The beans inside are fermented, dried and shipped across the world to make chocolate.

Read the sign to find out what the Aztecs put in their chocolate drinks to make them hot!

....

↑ Cocoa tree with pods.

COCONUT (H.12)

Sweets, coconut milk, doormats, face cream, food, potting compost and hair gel all come from coconut palms which grow in tropical places round the world.

↑ Coconut palm.

Can you see the RICE for their rice crispies?

H.12

H.13

OIL PALM (H.12)

Palm oil is squeezed from the seeds of the oil palm. Palm oil is used in some of the cakes and pies we buy, as well as in soap and make-up. Millions of oil palms have been planted in the tropics to supply oil for people the world over.

↑ Oil palms and oil drums.

RICE (H.13)

More rice is grown than nearly any other food. Rice feeds half the people in the world every single day – that's around 1.5 million tonnes of rice! Rice often grows in water.

↑ Rice growing in a rice paddy.

DIGGER FACTS!

DIGGER ON PALMS AND RICE

Did you know?
Wax polish for cars and shoes is made from the wax found on the upper surface of the leaves of the carnauba wax palm.

Did you know?
We see a 'man in the moon', but the Japanese see a 'rabbit in the moon'! Look for the rabbit in the Shimenawa (Japanese rice straw sculpture).

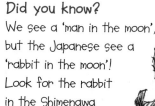

Where are the plants we get COFFEE and SUGAR from?

H.14

WHAT'S IN A CUP OF SWEET COFFEE?

COFFEE (H.14)

Coffee beans are found inside red coffee 'cherries'. These are often picked by hand.

↑ Coffee 'cherries'.

↑ Coffee beans and powder.

SUGAR CANE (H.16)

Sugar cane is a type of grass with stems about 5cm thick. The canes are crushed and the sugar is extracted with water. The solution is then evaporated, leaving a sticky brown liquid, called molasses, and crystals of raw sugar.

Yams and purple Malabar spinach are types of tropical...

....

(H.15)

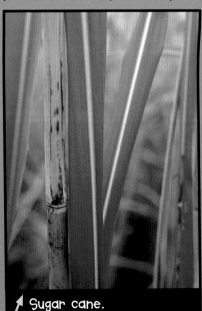

↑ Sugar cane.

Alan, look! I've found the BANANAS.

Help Alan and Enid find the JABOTICABA (the jabotiwhati?) fruit.

↓ Bananas growing on the stem.

BANANAS (H.18)

Bananas grow pointing upwards – how strange! There are hundreds of different sorts; long, short, yellow, even red. Some are eaten raw, some cooked and some made into beer. Use the leaves as plates and cups (saves on the washing up)!

TROPICAL FRUITS (H.19)

You probably recognise a juicy mango, but have you seen the fruits of the jaboticaba tree, that look like huge blackcurrants? You could be the first to recognise this fruit when it arrives in our supermarkets one day.

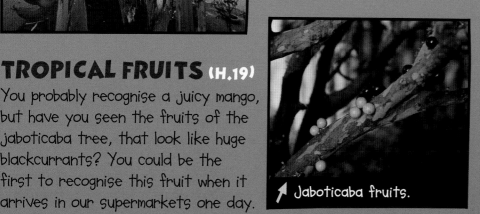

↑ Jaboticaba fruits.

DIGGER FACTS!

DIGGER DIGS FOR FRUIT

The Big Fight
Breadfruit are round, starchy fruits that can be roasted, boiled or fried.

Captain Bligh was carrying breadfruit plants from Tahiti to the West Indies on his ship, the Bounty, when the famous mutiny of 1789 took place.

Soppy ice cream
Soursop is a spiny fruit that makes a delicious ice cream.

REALLY USEFUL PLANTS!

↓ Bamboo, 'plant of a thousand uses'.

BAMBOO (H.20)

Half the world's people use bamboo – for homes and furniture, food and fuel, musical instruments and medicine, paper and poles, toys and tools, scaffolding and suspension bridges.

DYES (ANNATTO) (H.25)

The red dye called annatto, which comes from the seedpods of the bixa tree, is used to colour food as well as lipstick, so next time you eat red or orange sweets, think of the tree thousands of miles away in the hot, steamy tropics that grew the colour for you.

What fruits grow near the ground and look like giant yellow pine cones?
....

↑ The bixa tree with red seedpods used for annatto dye.

Can you help them find VANILLA?

ON THE CORNER, THEN SPICES WITH PEPPER VINES AND CLIMBING VANILLA ORCHIDS.

SPICES

PEPPER (H.23)

White and black peppercorns come from the red fruits of a climbing vine (Piper nigrum) in tropical Asia. Black peppercorns are made by drying the unripe fruits. White peppercorns are made by removing the red skin.

↗ Pepper on the vine.

VANILLA (H.23)

The vanilla orchid is grown for the pods which flavour vanilla ice cream. The pods have to be picked, sweated in the sun, then dried

↗ The vanilla orchid.

for months before they have any flavour. Most vanilla flavouring we eat now is made synthetically.

↗ The spice boat.

DIGGER FACTS!

DIGGER'S USEFUL PLANT FACTS

Madagascan periwinkle
The pink-flowered Madagascan periwinkle is used to treat childhood leukaemia.

Cashews
Cashew nuts hang below the large, red, pear-shaped fruits of the cashew tree.

JAUNTS IN THE JUNGLE

SEARCHING THE TROPICS

Alan and Enid have searched the Humid Tropics for the plants they needed. See if you can find them all.

PAPYRUS
PALM
MANGROVE
PAPRIKA
HORSERADISH TREE
PAPAYA
MANGO
CASSAVA
WATER CHESTNUT
COFFEE
SUGAR
BANANA
BIXA
PEPPER
VANILLA
COLA
CHEWING GUM
TIMBER
RUBBER
CHOCOLATE
COCONUT
PALM OIL
RICE
JABOTICABA

A	S	D	F	G	H	J	K	L	H	P	H	A
R	T	P	E	P	P	E	R	Y	U	A	O	D
A	S	P	A	L	M	O	I	L	X	P	R	D
C	V	B	N	P	A	P	R	I	K	A	S	C
D	F	G	H	A	Y	Q	B	A	A	A	Y	E
T	Y	U	N	L	V	R	A	A	A	A	R	O
C	A	S	I	M	V	M	U	B	C	V	A	C
R	H	C	O	L	A	O	I	S	M	C	D	O
W	R	E	U	H	J	N	J	U	A	A	I	L
T	A	A	W	G	P	Q	G	Y	N	S	S	A
B	F	T	T	I	M	B	E	R	G	S	H	T
G	G	Y	E	Y	N	U	U	H	O	A	T	E
H	W	H	I	R	A	G	U	S	P	V	R	C
Y	E	R	Y	U	C	O	G	I	L	A	E	I
Y	V	O	T	O	R	H	R	U	B	B	E	R
U	F	C	O	F	F	E	E	O	M	A	H	U
O	C	Q	E	Q	T	P	T	S	B	N	Y	Y
W	T	R	C	O	C	O	N	U	T	A	T	I
S	H	O	T	W	Y	Q	C	E	V	N	R	P
Z	J	A	B	O	T	I	C	A	B	A	U	Q
R	T	U	O	V	A	N	I	L	L	A	C	T

Need a clue? Don't forget to read diagonally as well as up, down, forwards and backwards.

COLOUR ME IN

HIDDEN BIRDS
How many White Eye birds can you see hopping around the page?
....

Fact check!

How many Sulawesi White Eyes have been released into the Humid Tropics Biome? ....

In what year was Captain Bligh transporting bread-fruit from Tahiti? ....

What letters help you to choose carefully grown timber? ....

(Answers at the back of the book.)

I want to find some POMEGRANATES for the fruit bowl.

W.01

I need some kitchen herbs. THYME would be fine.

W.02

THE WARM TEMPERATE REGIONS

THE WARM TEMPERATE BIOME (W.01)

Mediterranean countries, California (across the Atlantic) and South Africa (below the equator) all have a warm temperate climate with hot, dry summers and winter rain – despite the fact that they're so far apart.

↓ A golden line of olive oil...

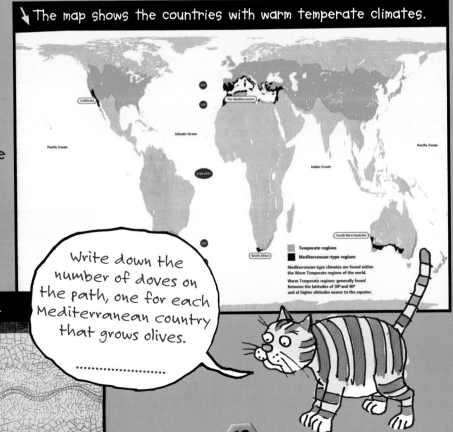

↘ The map shows the countries with warm temperate climates.

California

40°

30°

The Mediterranean

Pacific Ocean

Atlantic Ocean

equator

Indian Ocean

Pacific Ocean

30°

South West Australia

South Africa

■ Temperate regions
■ Mediterranean-type regions

Mediterranean-type climates are found within the Warm Temperate regions of the world.

Warm Temperate regions: generally found between the latitudes of 30° and 40° and at higher altitudes nearer to the equator.

Write down the number of doves on the path, one for each Mediterranean country that grows olives.

....

SUN FACTOR (W.02)

Travellers use sun cream, bottled water and walking shoes, but plants cope with the sun, lack of summer water, and things that bite by having small, pale or waxy leaves, scented oils, hairs and even spines.

↑ Typical small-leaved plants.

Look for CAROB – it tastes a bit like chocolate.

MEDITERRANEAN HERBS (W.02)

Small leaves and scented oil protect thyme from sun and fires. In the past people used thyme for its antiseptic properties, but now it's mostly used for flavour. You can grow it in the garden.

↑ Scented thyme.

CAROB TREE (W.02)

Carob seeds are used as a chocolate or coffee substitute. Also called locust beans, these might be what John the Baptist ate in the Bible story – not real locusts at all!

↑ Carob tree.

DIGGER FACTS!

DIGGER'S MEDITERRANEAN FACTS

Noah's ark
Cypress wood does not rot easily. Noah's ark was said to have been made of it.

Strange but true
The flowers of the fig tree are found inside the fruits.

Pomegranates
Pomegranates have a little crown shape at the end – just like a royal crown.

I'm looking for SAGE for my herb stuffing

They'll want some pretty PROTEA flowers with petals like bird feathers.

W.03

VISIT SOUTH AFRICA...

THE FYNBOS (W.03)

The Fynbos area of South Africa contains thousands of rare plants, including proteas, heathers and restios; 5,000 of them are found only in this one place. Eden's partners Fauna and Flora International are working to look after these plants and their endangered 'fine bush' home.

↑ The reed–like restios.

↓ Proteas in bloom.

NAMAQUALAND (W.03)

The red, dry desert of Namaqualand, South Africa, contains millions of seeds which lie waiting for rain. After a shower – pow! up come millions of colourful daisies which quickly make more seeds to return to the soil and wait for the next rain.

↑ Daisies of the desert – Namaqualand.

Name the place in South Africa where the land bakes to 50°C in the summer and freezes in winter.

Little ....

I've heard the AGAVE is a useful plant. Can you see it?

W.04

... AND CALIFORNIA

SCRUBBY SAGES
(W.04)

Sage leaves drop off when it gets really dry and regrow when it rains. Scented oil in the plants helps the bushes to burn when fires rage. They quickly grow again when the fire has passed.

↑ Californian sage scrub.

↑ Agave in the semi-desert.

SPIKY AGAVE (W.04)

The cactus-like agaves store gallons of moisture in their leaves. Agaves are used for their fibre (for brushes, sacking and twine) and some types have flowers that are made into soap. Most famously agave is used to make tequila.

DIGGER FACTS!

DIGGER GOES TO CALIFORNIA

Cowboys
'Chaparro', or scrub oak, gave its name to the chaparral area and to the 'chaps' worn by riders to protect their legs when riding through it.

... and Indians

The Native Americans who reached California about 15,000 years ago found so many wild plants and animals to eat that they had no need to develop farming.

Can you spot the TOBACCO? Enid and Alan don't need it – they don't smoke.

I'm looking for KIWI FRUITS and PEACHES.

W.05

W.06

CROPS AND CULTIVATION

CROPS FOR SHOPS (W.05)

Hot, dry regions are made lush and green to grow supermarket salads, fruits and other crops year-round. How? By controlling pests and diseases and by drawing up vast quantities of water from an underground supply that cannot last for ever.

↑ A Mediterranean scene.

↑ These life-like pigs are made from cork oak branches.

WHAT A CORKER (W.07)

The cork oak, unlike most other trees, regrows its bark after it has been stripped off, so using real corks doesn't destroy cork trees. Looking after cork oak forests also protects the rare birds that live in them.

What animal feeds on the acorns of the cork oak tree before becoming food itself?

....

I need some CORK for my wine bottles.

W.07

W.13

KIWI FRUITS (W.06)

These New Zealand fruits are named after the flightless, fluffy bird that lives there – the kiwi. Kiwi fruits first came from China, which is why they are sometimes called Chinese gooseberries.

↑ Kiwi fruit.

SUCCULENT PEACHES (W.06)

Peaches first came from China too. The ones without a furry skin are called nectarines. When you next eat a peach, try opening the stone. The kernel inside is like an almond – peach trees are closely related to almond trees. (Warning: don't eat peach stones. They could be poisonous.)

↑ Peach tree with fruit.

DIGGER FACTS!

DIGGER ON THE CORK OAK FORESTS

Black Vulture

Rare wildlife Cork oak forests provide a home for many creatures, including the Iberian lynx, the rare black vulture and the short-toed eagle.

Where are the ORANGES?

I'd rather look for GRAPES (to make wine)!

W.11

TUTTI FRUTTI

PEPPERS (W.08)

Like tomatoes, peppers are in fact fruits, and come in many colours. The peppery taste ranges in heat from mild to very hot, due to a natural chemical, capsaicin, found in the inner wall of the fruit.

↑ Peppers (or capsicums).

What am I? Sharp but smooth like a rugby ball, add an 'ade' and I'm bubbly and sweet.
....

↑ Orange trees.

ORANGES (W.10)

Oranges are citrus fruits and have many close relations such as lemons, limes, grapefruits, clementines and satsumas, along with less well-known ones, such as tangelos. Citrus fruit oils are used in scent and cleaning products.

DIGGER FACTS!

DIGGER DIGGING IN THE MED

Did you know?
Navel oranges are so named because they look as if they have belly buttons.

Did you know?
Basil, a herb that is grown in the Mediterranean, first came from India.

Did you know?
The ugli fruit is a cross between a tangerine and a grapefruit.

Can you see PEPPERS growing – or is it the wrong time of year?

W.10   W.08

THIS SECTION (THEY'RE NOT ALWAYS IN THE SAME PLACE).

DIONYSUS (W.11)

The big bronze bull is Dionysus, the Greek god who started life as god of horticulture and nature. Then he got keen on one plant – the grape – and its product, wine. After this he became god of festivities and wild parties.

VINES (W.11)

Vines produce a wide range of different sorts of grape. Some types are eaten raw, some are made into wine and others are dried to give us currants and raisins.

↑ Grapes.

↑ Dionysus and other strange revellers amongst the grape vines.

25

I need TOMATOES for my tomato sauce!

W.14

W.12

BEANS AND TOMATOES

↑ Bags of beans.

BEANS (W.12)

Beans, peas, lentils etc. are all known as pulses. As well as providing protein-packed food in their pods, these plants have specialised roots which can take nitrogen into the soil from the air around us. This improves the soil for the next lot of crops to be planted there.

What crop, grown in Africa, is used to make beer as well as bread?

....

(W.15)

↑ Ripe tomatoes.

TOMATOES (W.14)

The Spanish Conquistadors brought tomatoes to Europe from South America in the sixteenth century. People wouldn't eat them at first, because they thought they were poisonous.

I'm looking for BEANS.

They need cornflakes, too, so look for MAIZE.

W.15

MAIZE

↙ Maize (corn on the cob).

A-MAIZE-ING BUT TRUE

What plant is found in popcorn, shoe polish, fireworks, marshmallows, ice cream and paint? It's maize.

MAIZE IN CENTRAL AMERICA (W.15)

People have been eating maize for over 7,000 years. It comes from Mexico where the Aztecs worshipped maize gods Cinteotl and Xilonen, in the belief that the gods were responsible for looking after it and helping it to grow.

MAIZE IN AFRICA (W.15)

QPM, quality protein maize, has been bred to contain more nutrients than ordinary maize. In Ghana, it's called 'Obatampa' (good nursing mother).

MAIZE IN EUROPE (W.15)

We eat maize as sweet corn, cornflakes and popcorn, ground up in polenta, or as the flour in Mexican tortillas. We use cornflour to thicken sauces.

DIGGER FACTS!

DIGGER DIGGING ON GRAINS

Did you know?
If you ate cornflakes, rice crispies, oat crunchies or puffed wheat for breakfast, you were eating grass!

Did you know?
Tef, possibly the smallest grain in the world, is grown and eaten in Ethiopia, often as flour in a sort of pancake.

I need COTTON for my T-shirt and jeans.

SKiRT ROUND THE iSLAND WiTH iTS COTTON (iN SUMMER) TO FACE THE PERFUME

THE SCENT OF THE MEDITERRANEAN

↑ Cotton 'bolls'.

↑ Cotton fabric.

OLIVES (W.17)

People have been cultivating olive trees in Mediterranean countries for 10,000 years. The black olives on your pizza are simply riper than green olives, but both are preserved in salty water. Olive oil has had many uses, in religious rituals (it is mentioned in the Bible), in oil lamps, medicine and cosmetics, as well as in food.

What is the name of the fruits of this tree, Oval and green, good for you, good for me? Pick them, squeeze them, lots of toil. The result: a healthy, golden oil.

....

COTTON (W.16)

Cotton clothes are made from the spun seed fibres of the cotton plant. These long fibres are also made into fishing nets, tents, nappies, wallpaper, bandages, rope, sheets and even paper.

↗ Olives turning from green to black.

Look for OLIVES for olive oil!

I've found some SCENTED PLANTS for perfume.

W.18

PERFUME (W.18)

Why do flowers so often smell lovely? Because they make perfume to attract bees. In their search for nectar the bees carry pollen from one flower to another, pollinating them so they can make seeds.

↑ Geranium, used for perfume oil.

CLEOPATRA (W.18)

Cleopatra liked perfume. She wore rose and violet perfume on her hands and almond, cinnamon and orange perfume on her feet.

↑ Sweet-scented roses.

DIGGER FACTS!

DIGGER SNIFFS IT OUT

Did you know?
Jasmine, roses, geraniums and lavender are the flowers most often used in scent and bathroom smellies.

Did you know?
We can detect over 10,000 smells.

Did you know?
Your sense of smell is linked to the part of your brain that handles memory and emotion.

FUN IN THE SUN

SEARCHING THE WARM TEMPERATE REGIONS

Alan and Enid have searched the Warm Temperate Regions for all sorts of plants. See if you can find them here.

COLOUR ME IN

Unscramble these words to find the plant names.

NOCTOT
EVOIL
EMHYT
BAROC
GENORA
OTAMTO
ZEIMA
EPRAG
TEAORP
OCACBOT
SBAEN
SPREPEP
KORC
GASE
WIIK
CHEAP
EAGVA

HIDDEN GECKOS

How many geckos can you see scooting around the page?

....

PLANT CHECK

Tick off all the plants you've spotted during your sunny stroll through the Warm Temperate Biome.

- [ ] P.19 THYME W.02
- [ ] P.19 CAROB W.02
- [ ] P.19 POMEGRANATES W.02
- [ ] P.20 PROTEA W.03
- [ ] P.21 SAGE W.04
- [ ] P.21 AGAVE W.04
- [ ] P.22 CORK W.07
- [ ] P.23 KIWI FRUITS W.06
- [ ] P.23 PEACHES W.06
- [ ] P.23 TOBACCO W.13
- [ ] P.24 PEPPERS W.08
- [ ] P.24 ORANGES W.10
- [ ] P.25 GRAPES W.11
- [ ] P.26 BEANS W.12
- [ ] P.26 TOMATOES W.14
- [ ] P.27 MAIZE W.15
- [ ] P.28 COTTON W.16
- [ ] P.28 OLIVES W.17
- [ ] P.29 SCENTED FLOWERS W.1

Fact check!

Which wood might Noah have used for the Ark?

 ....

Which fruit is a cross between a tangerine and a grapefruit?

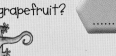 ....

How many smells can we detect?

 ....

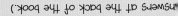

(Answers at the back of the book.)

THE OUTDOOR BIOME

If you are starting this section from the Biomes rather than the Visitors' Centre, go straight to the next page.

I want blue dye but these WOAD flowers are yellow!

The ferns will turn into COAL – in a few million years' time!

0.01

0.04

0.05

↘ The plants for taste garden (0.06).

Name the feathery-looking plants that were around before the days of the dinosaurs.

....

PLANTS FOR FOOD...

THE OUTDOOR BIOME

Outside you'll find plants from Britain and other places (such as parts of India, America and Russia) that share our temperate climate. Several crops in our Outdoor Biome move plots each year so they may not always be where you expect them; they'll be marked here with an **M**.

↑ Potatoes.

↑ Potato tops with flowers.

POTATOES (0.03)

Potatoes come from the same family as tomatoes. We eat the tubers that grow under the ground. First discovered in the Andes in South America, potatoes are one of the biggest food crops in the world. How do you like yours?

(speech bubble) I fancy some chips! Where do I get POTATOES?

...AND COLOUR

GARDEN FLOWERS
(0.04)

Garden flowers all have wild ancestors. Some are bred deliberately, but others occur by accident. Our beautiful summer dahlias are great-grandchildren of the wild dahlia from Mexico.

↗ Dahlia 'Juul Allstar'.

COLOURS AND DYES
(0.05)

Several plants, including the woad used by ancient Britons, contain a dye called indigo. It appears after processing, when the leaves are mixed with wood ash, hot water and other ingredients. The dyed cloth is yellow at first but turns blue when it makes contact with the air. Magic!

↗ A vat of Indigo dye.

DIGGER FACTS!

DIGGER DIGS IN THE VEGGIE PATCH

True or false?

1 Carrots help you see in the dark.

2 Spinach makes you strong.

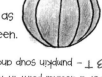

3 Pumpkins can be eaten as well as carved for Halloween.

(upside-down answers)

1 T – carrots contain vitamin A, which is good for the eyesight.

2 F – spinach contains less iron than was once thought. The confusion was caused when someone put a decimal point in the wrong place!

3 T – pumpkin soup and pumpkin pie are both delicious.

Pretty blue-flowered LINSEED can be made into floor cleaner!

I can smell the LAVENDER for my shower gel from here.

0.08 M

0.07

HeAD FOR THE bEE, THEN MAKE YOUR WAY THROUGH THE GATE TOWARDS THE GiANT

WHAT'S GROWING HERE?

PLANTS FOR TOMORROW'S INDUSTRIES

(0.08)M

Plastic can be made from plants as well as from fossil fuels such as oil. For example, maize plant stems can be made into the plant plastic that disposable knives and forks are made of. Carrier bags that are made from plant plastic rot down on the compost heap. As well as plastic, plants can be made into paint thinner, floor cleaner, car door panels, railway grease and all sorts of unusual products.

↑ A tree made from plant plastic.

What is the giant insect in the pollination garden?

....

↑ Bombus the bee.

34

APPLES for the fruit bowl, where are youuuuu?

0.09 0.10

HOW MANY APPLES? (0.07)

There are over 2,000 cultivated varieties of apples. Here in our Garden of Eden you can find two – Blenheim Orange and Blackamoor Red – watched over by the beautiful Eve, who is made from wood, mud and grass.

↑ Lavender bushes.

LAVENDER (0.09)

Lavender flowers in the summer. Its name comes from the Latin 'lavare', which means to wash. (So do the words laundry and lavatory.) Lavender is mainly used as a perfume, but it also has great healing properties. It's used to flavour cakes and ice cream too.

↑ Eve and the artists.

DIGGER FACTS!

DIGGER GETS INTO POLLINATION (0.10)

The go-between
How do plants get together to reproduce? Colour, scent and nectar all attract insects which carry the pollen from one flower to another.

Insects, good or bad?
Many food plants need pollinating by insects, so think twice before swatting bugs. Your lunch is at stake!

SUNFLOWERS, BEER AND A NICE CUP OF TEA

↑ Turn the handle to watch Mike Chaikin's metal sunflowers follow the sun.

SUNFLOWERS (0.14) M

Mike Chaikin, a Cornish sculptor, made the sunflower sculpture after discovering "a piece of film showing time-lapse photography of sunflowers tracking the sun through the day, taken by Sarah Darwin – Charles Darwin's great-great-granddaughter."

SUNFLOWER OIL (0.14) M

The oil from sunflower seeds can be used in racing-car engines as well as in the margarine that we spread on our bread. Have a look in the little window in Mike's sculpture to see what else sunflowers are used for.

Help Alan find the HOPS for beer and he might change his mind!

TEA (O.13)

Next to the giant tea leaf are tea bushes from India. Tea is made from the young leaves. Prem Wallia, from the Kotada Tea Estate in India, came over to show us how to grow and pick our tea.

↑ The tea garden.

BEER AND BREWING (O.12)

Look at the carved hop poles to find what's used in beer-making: barley, wheat, hops, yeast, a copper kettle, a fish (its swim bladder is added to beer to clear it), the chemical formula for alcohol and one more...

↑ Hop poles with real hops growing in the background.

DIGGER FACTS!

DIGGER ON CORNISH CROPS

Did you know? Spring comes early to Cornwall, so traditionally Cornish farmers could sell certain vegetables, such as cauliflowers, earlier than growers in colder parts of Britain.

ECHINACEA (purple cone flowers) can be used as medicine. **0.19**

I fancy some bread! Where do I get WHEAT? **0.18**

BREAD AND ROPE

The metal giant.

HEMP (**0.16**)

Canvas sails and ships' ropes,
Tough clothes and bank notes,
Oils and cords, insulation boards,
Soap and Bibles, old masters and fibres.
All this from hemp. Hemp has 25,000 uses.
Here we've used it to make a rope fence.

PLANTS FOR ROPE AND FIBRE (**0.18**)

Strong plant fibres make strong rope. The metal giant made by local artist George Fairhurst will show you how tough a rope can be!

↑ The hemp fence, a strong barrier made from plant stems.

Name one of the plants that we use for making ropes.

....

I've spotted the ROPE plants. Now we can make a washing line.

0.16

0.17 M

WHEAT (0.17) M

Bread flour is ground from bread wheat and pasta flour is ground from durum wheat. Wheat – usually in the form of bread – is the staple food of a third of the world's population. Two hundred years ago a worker in Britain would spend half his week's wages on bread.

Wheat ready for harvesting.

STEPPE AND PRAIRIE (0.19)

The purple cone flower, Echinacea, now sold in a medicine to boost the immune system, comes from the prairies of North America, where native Americans had been using it for centuries as a medicine.

The purple cone flower, Echinacea.

DIGGER FACTS!

DIGGER ON THE PRAIRIE

Nowhere to hide
Check out the burnt trees in the prairie exhibit. The prairies were probably cleared of trees by native Americans burning them to make hunting easier. The bison couldn't hide behind those stumps!

Hardwearing jeans
The original jeans were made of hemp fabric. It would have taken a long time for them to wear out!

I need to gather FUEL for the fire.

GORSE was once used for fuel in Cornwall.

0.20

AS YOU LEAVE THE PRAIRIE LOOK OUT FOR THE 'INDUSTRIAL PLANT' BEFORE GOING UP

STORIES BY THE FIRESIDE

DON'T BE A FOSSIL

David Kemp's 'industrial plant' sculpture shows 'fuels past'. Burning fossil fuels, like coal and oil, pumps carbon dioxide into the air and contributes to global warming.

PLANTS FOR FUEL (0.20)

At Eden we're growing willow, poplar and a grass called miscanthus for fuel. These plants take in the same amount of carbon dioxide when growing as they give out when they're burning. This is called 'carbon neutral'.

⬆ David Kemp's 'industrial plant'.

⬇ Miscanthus.

Look in Wild Cornwall for a stone book. What is the name of the wild plant inside?

....

⬆ Gorse.

I just want a rest and a STORY.

↑ Stone hand.

WILD CORNWALL (O.22)

Up here you can discover the real Cornwall of stone walls and gorse and Cornish wild flowers. Cornwall's a magical place, so look out for a poem in slate, books in stone and clouds beneath your feet...

STORYTELLING AT EDEN (O.21)

If plants are kept alive in your memory by stories, they have a better chance of being kept alive when they're growing in the ground, too. Listen out for storytellers as you go round Eden. It can be nice to sit down and listen after all that walking!

↑ Storyteller at Eden.

DIGGER FACTS!

DIGGER CHASES CLOUDS

Cloud chamber
Whatever is passing overhead while you sit in the cloud chamber is magically projected on to the floor. Digger saw birds and clouds going by. Shame there were no flying rabbits!

THE OUTDOOR BIOME

EDEN VILLAGE: PIT STOP CHALLENGE

Take a breather and check out where you've been and what you've seen ... and if you've done it, tick the box.

1. ☐ **WALKED ROUND THE LAKE**
2. ☐ **BEEN ON THE LAND TRAIN**
3. ☐ **SEEN OR HEARD A BIRD IN THE HUMID TROPICS BIOME**
4. ☐ **LEARNT SOMETHING FROM A GUIDE**
5. ☐ **HEARD A STORY**
6. ☐ **WALKED PAST A GIANT BRONZE BULL IN THE WARM TEMPERATE BIOME**
7. ☐ **LISTENED TO SOME MUSIC**
8. ☐ **SMELT SOMETHING NICE**
9. ☐ **SAT UNDER A GIANT TEA LEAF**
10. ☐ **RECYCLED A CAN**
11. ☐ **FOUND RED, YELLOW, PINK AND BLUE FLOWERS IN WILD CORNWALL**
12. ☐ **AND OF COURSE: SEEN ALAN, ENID, DIGGER AND THE CAT.**

A PICTURE OF ME AT EDEN

Draw a picture or take a photo to put in here to personalise your guide book.

Plant diary

Write down which plants you have used today (and not just the ones you have eaten).

Breakfast: _____

Morning: _____

Lunchtime: _____

Afternoon: _____

Supper: _____

Bathroom: _____

Bed: _____

DRAW A LINE TO MATCH THE PLANT TO THE PRODUCT.

NAME THAT CAT

Look back through this book at your answers to my questions and jot them down on the dotted lines below. (Ask a guide for help if you didn't find them all.) Take the first letter of the ones marked with a star and rearrange them to find my name.
Clue: It tastes a bit like chocolate.

HUMID TROPICS

P.2...
P.5...
P.6...
★ P.8...
★ P.10...
P.12...
P.14...

WARM TEMPERATE

P.18...
P.20. Little
P.22...
P.24...
P.26...
★ P.28...

OUTDOOR

P.32...
★ P.34...
★ P.36...
P.38...
P.40...

[ ] [ ] [ ] [ ] [ ]

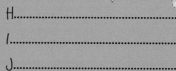

WRITE AN ABC OF EDEN

Write down plants starting with each letter of the alphabet.

A...
B...
C...
D...
E...
F...
G...

H...
I...
J...
K...
L...
M...
N...
O...
P...

Q...
R...
S...
T...
U...
V...
W...
X. Xanthosoma
Y. Ylang ylang
Z. Zea mays

PLANT CHECK

Tick off all the plants you've spotted during your exploration of the Outdoor Biome.

- [ ] P.32 POTATOES 0.03m
- [ ] P.33 WOAD 0.05
- [ ] P.33 VEGETABLES 0.06
- [ ] P.34 LINSEED 0.08m
- [ ] P.35 LAVENDER 0.09
- [ ] P.35 APPLES 0.07
- [ ] P.36 SUNFLOWERS 0.14 m
- [ ] P.37 TEA 0.13
- [ ] P.37 HOPS 0.12m
- [ ] P.38 HEMP 0.16
- [ ] P.39 WHEAT 0.17m
- [ ] P.39 ECHINACEA 0.19
- [ ] P.40 MISCANTHUS 0.20

HIDDEN BUTTERFLIES

How many butterflies can you see flitting around these two pages?

....

Fact check!

What do insects carry from one plant to another to fertilise them?

....

What comes early to Cornwall?

....

What fabric were the original jeans made from?

....

43

(Answers at the back of the book.)

EDEN - THE FACTS

STRUCTURE
The Biome scaffolding was the largest free-standing scaffold ever built: 12 levels, 25m across, 46,000 poles, 368 km of it in all.

BIG PITCH
In the beginning the disused china clay pit was 60m deep and the area of 35 football pitches.

HUGE
There are 625 hexagons in all, the largest being 11 metres across.

DISASTER!
43 million gallons of water raining into the pit in 90 days meant that our engineers had to come up with a fantastic drainage system right from the start.

HEAVY
The covered Biomes sit on very solid foundations that weigh more than the Biomes themselves.

SIZE
The world's largest conservatories weigh only slightly more than the air they contain. The Tower of London could fit inside the Humid Tropics Biome.

PLANT TASTE
Different soil mixes are used in each area to make sure the plants have exactly what they need to grow best.

BUBBLES
Three layers of ETFE (ethylenetetrafluoroethylene) transparent foil form inflated pillows 2m deep in each of the hexagons. ETFE weighs less than 1% of the same area of glass.

STRENGTH
2,000 rock anchors were driven into the pit sides to stabilise them. A 'soup' of grass seed and plant food was sprayed onto the slopes to knit the surface together.

SOIL
In a pit with no soil the team had to make their own – 85,000 tonnes of it – using china clay waste and organic waste. The compost heap to beat them all!

TARZAN
You may see strings dangling from the taller trees; these are small pulley systems to put 'good' bugs into the canopy.

DIRT
1.8 million tonnes of dirt was shifted by 12 dumper trucks and 8 bulldozers in 6 months.

PESKY PESTS
We put 'good' bugs in the Biomes to eat the 'bad' bugs that eat the plants.

LARGEST
flowering plant at Eden: Titan Arum, Humid Tropics Biome.

RAREST
plant at Eden: Ebony, Tropical Islands, Humid Tropics.

BIGGEST WATER PLANT LEAF
at Eden: Victorian giant water lily, Humid Tropics Biome.

TALLEST
Tallest tree in Humid Tropics Biome: the kapok tree at 16 metres.

NOT A PLANT ZOO
We show you the plants of the world that we depend on but which most of us have never seen.

HOW MANY PLANTS?
In 2003: over 7,400 plants, of approximately 3,865 species.

SMELLIEST
flowering plant at Eden: Pelican flower, Humid Tropics Biome.

GIGANTIC LEAF
The biggest leaf at Eden: Gunnera manicata (giant rhubarb) in the Outdoor Biome, by the lake.

BUZZ OFF!
We also put light boxes in some areas, which emit UV light at night to catch moths and mosquitoes.

YUM
See if you can spot the birds, lizards and geckos in the Humid Tropics Biome. They are there to eat the bugs.

MISTY MOUNTAINS
Fine spray from the misting nozzles keeps the humidity between 60% and 90% in the Humid Tropics Biome – just right for the plants.

HEATING UP
Temperatures in the Biomes are automatically controlled. The main heating source for both Biomes (even in winter) is the sun, with extra heating from air-handling units around each Biome.

SCORCHING
Unlike glass, ETFE transmits ultraviolet rays, which means you can get a suntan indoors. Don't forget to cover up.

COOLING DOWN
Air inside the Biomes is circulated by large grey boxes with two pipes which are positioned around the perimeter of each Biome.

QUIZZICLE:

HUMID TROPICS

1. Why are there birds in the Humid Tropics Biome?
a. To look beautiful
b. To eat the bugs
c. To create air movement with the flapping of their wings

2. Which plant did the Ancient Egyptians use to write on?
a. Papyrus
b. Rubber tree
c. Mangrove

3. What plant has the biggest seeds in the world?
a. The orchid
b. The elephant tree
c. The coco-de-mer

4. What tree gave us chewing gum?
a. Gorilla
b. Armadillo
c. Sapodilla

5. What is another name for a medicine man?
a. Showman
b. Shaman
c. Shoeman

6. Rubber can be made from
a. The liquid from the trunk of a tree?
b. A tropical fruit?
c. The root of a vine?

7. What palm gives us car polish?
a. Oil palm
b. Coconut palm
c. Carnauba wax palm

8. Soursop is a tropical fruit used for making
a. Ice cream?
b. Soup?
c. Sourdough bread?

9. Which flower has helped to save children's lives?
a. Madagascan periwinkle
b. The butterfly bush
c. The bucket orchid

WARM TEMPERATE

1. Why do many plants in the Med. have small leaves?
a. To help shed water
b. To prevent the plants from drying out
c. To keep the wind off

2. Where do you find the flowers of the fig tree?
a. Inside the fruits
b. On the trunks
c. On the ground

3. What South African flowers have petals like bird feathers?
a. Restios
b. Ericas
c. Proteas

4. What plants store gallons of moisture in their leaves?
a. Bananas
b. Agaves
c. Heathers

5. What birds live in the cork oak forests in the Mediterranean?
a. Parrots
b. Robins
c. Black Vultures

6. How did the navel orange get its name?
a. Because sailors ate it
b. Because it is grown in a village called Navel
c. Because the fruits look as if they have belly buttons

7. What plant can be made into popcorn, paint and cornflakes?
a. Maize
b. Wheat
c. Barley

8. What plant made lamp oil and now makes cooking oil?
a. Sunflower
b. Olive
c. Maize

9. How many different types of smells can we detect?
a. 10
b. 100
c. 10,000

OUTDOOR BIOME

1. What British plant gives us blue dye?
a. Sweet peas
b. Woad
c. Ferns

2. Which plants made our coal?
a. Ferns
b. Oak trees
c. Cabbages

3. What do we get bread and pasta from?
a. Barley
b. Oats
c. Wheat

4. How many different types of apples are there?
a. 20
b. 200
c. 2000

5. Lavender comes from a Latin word meaning
a. To smell?
b. To taste?
c. To wash?

6. Racing car engine oil can be made from
a. Sunflowers?
b. Rubber?
c. Honey?

7. Tea grows in
a. Iceland?
b. India?
c. Wales?

8. Potatoes first came from
a. Spain?
b. Africa?
c. South America?

9. What Cornish plant was used as a fuel?
a. Wild asparagus
b. Red campion
c. Gorse

The answers are at the back of the book.

ANSWERS

QUIZZICLE P.46

HTB
1b, 2a, 3c, 4c, 5b, 6a, 7c, 8a, 9a

WTB
1b, 2a, 3c, 4b, 5c, 6c, 7a, 8b, 9c

OB
1b, 2a, 3c, 4c, 5c, 6a, 7b, 8c, 9b

CAT QUESTIONS THROUGHOUT

Humid Tropics

p.2 Tropics Trader
p.5 Star fruit
p.6 Kapok
p.8 Artifice
p.10 Chillies
p.12 Vegetables
p.14 Pineapple

Warm Temperate

p.18 Twenty-two
p.20 Little Karoo
p.22 Pig
p.24 Lemon
p.26 Sorghum
p.28 Olives

Outdoor Biome

p.32 Ferns
p.34 Bee
p.36 Roots
p.38 Hemp and sisal
p.40 Gentian

NAME THAT CAT
CAROB

THE OUTDOOR BIOME P.42

MATCH THE PLANT TO THE PRODUCT.

Rubber tree = rubber gloves
coconut = mat
grapes = wine
cotton = T-shirt
wheat = bread

Fact check!
Pollen
Spring
Hemp

HIDDEN BUTTERFLIES 20

FUN IN THE SUN P.30

SEARCHING THE MEDITERRANEAN CLIMATES

THYME — GRAPE
CAROB — COTTON
PROTEA — BEANS
SAGE — MAIZE
AGAVE — TOMATO
OLIVE — PEACH
KIWI
CORK
TOBACCO
PEPPERS
ORANGE

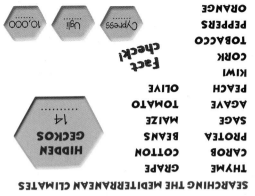

HIDDEN GECKOS 14

Fact check!
Cypress
Ugli
10,000

JAUNTS IN THE JUNGLE P.16

SEARCHING THE TROPICS

HIDDEN BIRDS 12

Fact check!
20
1789
FSC